Published by E.Stones, LLC
www.estonesllc.com

Edited by Kimberli Wilson

Cover and illustrations. Chris House Studio PaintedBlade, LLC.

Printed in the United States of America – St. Louis, Missouri

First Printing, 2020

ISBN-13: 978-1-7349985-1-1

I Am♥:

Everything They Said I Couldn't Be!

Written by
Haleigh A. Ingram

Dedication

To every young leader of tomorrow,
I pray this book inspires you as some of
our greatest leaders have inspired me.
Be Courageous, Be Responsible,
and Be YOU.

To my mommy, thank you for always
encouraging me to keep God first, pursue
my dreams and explore all my talents.

In Loving Memory of

My Grandfather's

Randolph Ingram Sr. & Lemuel Houston Jr.

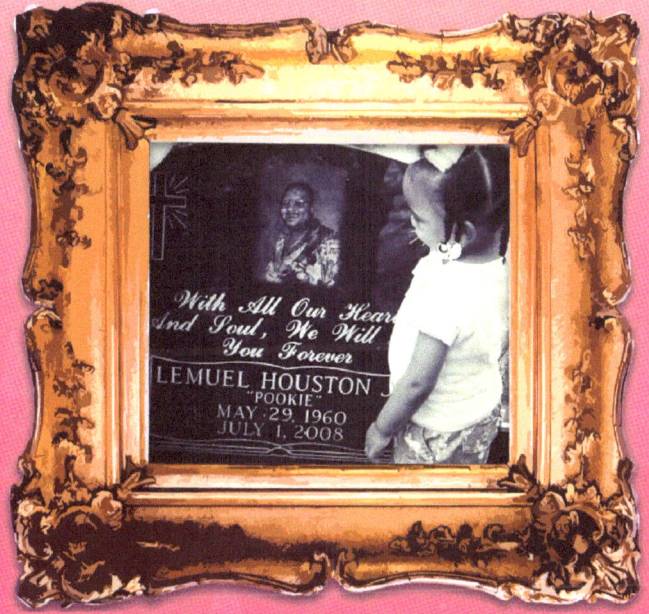

I Will Make You Both Proud...
Love Haleigh

I Am...

I was born into slavery in Eastern Maryland sometime between 1820 and 1821.

As a child, I was struck in the head with a weight that caused my skull to crack and ultimately caused me to start having seizures.

I escaped slavery yet I returned to Maryland in 1850 after learning that my niece would soon be auctioned off and sold as a slave.

1

I made 13 missions to rescue approximately 70 enslaved people, including my family and friends, using the net-work of antislavery activists and safe houses known as the Underground Railroad.

I earned the nickname "Moses" after the prophet Moses in the Bible who led his people to freedom.

I wore many hats: I was an active proponent of women's suffrage and I also worked for the Union Army as a cook as well as a nurse.

I Am...
Harriet Tubman!

"Every great dream begins with a dreamer.
Always remember, you have within you the strength, the patience,
and the passion to reach for the stars to change the world."
- Harriet Tubman

3

I Am...

My childhood gave me early experiences with racial discrimination and activism for racial equality.

I was an American activist in the civil rights movement and known for my pivotal role in the Montgomery bus boycott.

One day while heading home from work, I was asked to give up my seat to a white passenger on a segregated bus. I refused and therefore, I was arrested.

I didn't refuse to give my seat up because my feet were tired, I was a different kind of tired, I was tired of giving in.

My bravery led to nationwide efforts to end racial segregation. I was awarded the Dr. Martin Luther King Jr. Award by the National Association for the Advancement of Colored People as well as the Presidential Medal of Freedom and the Congressional Gold Medal.

The United States Congress has called me "The First Lady of Civil Rights" and "The Mother of the Freedom Movement".

I Am...
Rosa Parks!

"Our mistreatment was just not right, and I was tired of it."
- Rosa Parks

8

I Am...

I was born into slavery and sold at an auction at the age of nine, along with a flock of sheep, for $100.

I birthed 13 children, and witnessed most of them sold off to slavery.

I escaped slavery with my infant daughter to freedom in 1826.

After going to court to recover my son in 1828, I was one of the first black women to successfully challenge a white man in a United States court and win.

I was an African American abolitionist and women's rights activist best known for my speech on racial inequalities, "Ain't I A Woman?"; Delivered in 1851 at the Ohio Women's Rights Convention.

I was honored with an invitation to the White House and became involved with the Freedmen's Bureau, helping freed slaves find jobs and build new lives.

I Am...
Sojourner Truth!

"If the Lord comes and burns—as you say he will—I am not going away; I am going to stay here and stand the fire ... And Jesus will walk with me through the fire, and keep me from harm." —Sojourner Truth

11

12

I Am...

I was the first of my parent's children to be born free from slavery.

I suffered from a scalp ailment that resulted in my own hair loss.

I created specialized hair products for African American hair care and was one of the first American women to become a self-made millionaire.

I promoted my hair products by traveling around the country giving lecture-demonstrations and eventually established laboratories to manufacture cosmetics and conduct sales training for beauticians.

In 1913, I donated the largest amount of money by an African American toward the construction of an Indianapolis YMCA.

As a civil rights activist, in 1917 I was part of a delegation that traveled to the White House to petition President Woodrow Wilson to make lynching a federal crime.

I Am...
Madam C.J. Walker!

I had to make my own living and my own opportunity. But I made it! Don't sit down and wait for the opportunities to come. Get up and make them."
—Madam C.J. Walker

15

16

I Am...

I attended Harvard Law School. During my time on campus, I participated in demonstrations demanding that the school accept more students and professors of color.

I became a lawyer, an author and the First African American First Lady of the United States from 2009 to 2017.

When I became First Lady, I started the "Let's Move" campaign to help stop the United States childhood obesity epidemic.

I encouraged education for girls, championed for equal rights, advocated for American families in poverty, and pushed for healthy living and eating.

Many have called me a modern-day revolutionary woman.

I am happily married to the first African American President of the United States and we have two beautiful daughters.

I Am...
Michelle Obama!

"You may not always have a comfortable life and you will not always be able to solve all of the world's problems at once--but don't ever underestimate the importance you can have, because history has shown us that courage can be contagious and hope can take on a life of its own."
-Michelle Obama

I Am...

I was born and raised in St. Louis, MO.

I am the youngest member on my praise and worship team at church.

I am the founder of H.K. Community Action Program for Children and Families.

I love animals and hope to operate the world largest pet hospital and community center.

I am an honors student.

I love reading, writing and learning about my history.

I'm a natural gymnast and love to dance and sing.

21

I Am...
Haleigh Ingram!

"Let's not forget the fight that our ancestors fought, so that we can live and be free today."

I AM
Ms. Harriet Tubman.

I AM
Ms. Sojourner Truth.

I AM
Ms. Madame
C.J. Walker.

I AM
Ms. Rosa Parks!

I AM
Mrs. Michelle Obama.

I AM Ms. Haleigh Ingram.
And SO ARE YOU!

23

We have the Power to be who we want to be. All of these women and so many more made sacrifices so that we as little girls and young women of tomorrow can strive and reach our goals with confidence.

I chose this group of influential women because even in oppression they were BOLD and BRAVE. They broke down barriers and didn't let anything or anyone stop them. Every tear they shed and every battle they won should be celebrated daily.

I AM Everything each of them were told they couldn't be and SO ARE YOU!

XO XO,
Haleigh

My favorite poem I often recite at church and local events:

Hey Black Child
Do you know who you are
Who you really are
Do you know you can be
What you want to be
If you try to be
What you can be

Hey Black Child
Do you know where you are going
Where you're really going
Do you know you can learn
What you want to learn
If you try to learn
What you can learn

Hey Black Child
Do you know you are strong
I mean really strong
Do you know you can do
What you want to do
If you try to do
What you can do

Hey Black Child
Be what you can be
Learn what you must learn
Do what you can do
And tomorrow your nation
Will be what you want it to be

By Useni Eugene Perkins

25

About the Author

Haleigh Andrea Ingram is an energetic, ambitious 7-year old who's drive and passion to encourage others is far beyond her years. It was her idea to create the Haleigh Kares Foundation which caters to children in the inner cities as well as the local children's hospital intensive care units in St. Louis, MO.

After her mother started a children's boutique in her honor "Haleigh Kouture Kids", she decided to take it a step further and create a community for young entrepreneurs reminding them that "You Can Be Everything They Told Our Ancestors They Couldn't Be & More."

Haleigh wants to inspire the world and encourage youth to push pass all obstacles, pursue their dreams and spread love while doing so.

www.ingramcontent.com/pod-product-compliance
Lightning Source LLC
LaVergne TN
LVHW072056070426
835508LV00002B/124